Easy Classics for ALTO SAXOPHONE

With Piano Accompaniment

Piano Accompaniments by **Jannette Spitzer** and **Laura Spitzer**

Selected and Arranged by **Peter Spitzer**

The *Easy Classics* books were written to provide beginning to intermediate instrumentalists with an enjoyable introduction to some of the great classic melodies.

The flute, clarinet, alto sax, tenor sax, and trumpet parts are fully compatible, and may be played in any combination, with or without piano accompaniment. (Note to the pianist: Solo and duet parts are shown in the upper staff, in concert key. For some instruments, actual pitch may be in a lower octave.)

The violin book is transposed to keys suitable for that instrument, and has its own accompaniment.

Peter Spitzer

Contents

MEL BAY®

1 2 3 4 5 6 7 8 9 0

Ode to Joy
from Symphony #9

Ludwig van Beethoven (1770-1827)

3

Sleeping Beauty Waltz

from the ballet "Sleeping Beauty"

Peter Ilich Tchaikovsky (1843-1890)

Eine Kleine Nachtmusik

from Serenade K. 525

Wolfgang Amadeus Mozart (1756-1791)

Allegro moderato

7

8

Adagio
from Clarinet Concerto, K. 622

Wolfgang Amadeus Mozart (1756-1791)

Hungarian Dance #5

Johannes Brahms (1833-1897)

Emperor Hymn

Franz Joseph Haydn (1732-1809)

Maestoso

The Trout

Franz Schubert (1797-1828)

Moderato

Theme from Polovetsian Dances

from the opera "Prince Igor"

Alexander Borodin (1833-1887)

Scheherazade

Nicholas Rimsky-Korsakov (1844-1908)

Easy Classics for ALTO SAXOPHONE

With Piano Accompaniment

Includes works by:
Bach
Beethoven
Bizet
Borodin
Brahms
di Capua
Haydn
Mozart
Offenbach
Rimsky-Korsakov
Rossini
Schubert
Strauss
Tchaikovsky

Piano Accompaniments
by **Jannette Spitzer**
and **Laura Spitzer**

Selected and Arranged
by **Peter Spitzer**

MEL BAY ®

The *Easy Classics* books were written to provide beginning to intermediate instrumentalists with an enjoyable introduction to some of the great classic melodies.

The flute, clarinet, alto sax, tenor sax, and trumpet parts are fully compatible, and may be played in any combination, with or without piano accompaniment. (Note to the pianist: Solo and duet parts are shown in the upper staff, in concert key. For some instruments, actual pitch may be in a lower octave.)

The violin book is transposed to keys suitable for that instrument, and has its own accompaniment.

Peter Spitzer

Contents

Ode to Joy
from Symphony #9

Ludwig van Beethoven (1770-1827)

Sleeping Beauty Waltz
from the ballet "Sleeping Beauty"

Peter Ilich Tchaikovsky (1843-1890)

Alto sax 1

Alto sax 2

Eine Kleine Nachtmusik
from Serenade K. 525

Allegro moderato   Wolfgang Amadeus Mozart (1756-1791)

Adagio
from Clarinet Concerto, K. 622

Wolfgang Amadeus Mozart (1756-1791)

10

Hungarian Dance #5

Johannes Brahms (1833-1897)

Emperor Hymn

Maestoso

Franz Joseph Haydn (1732-1809)

14

15

The Trout

Franz Schubert (1797-1828)

Theme from Polovetsian Dances

from the opera "Prince Igor"

Alexander Borodin (1833-1887)

Scheherazade

Nicholas Rimsky-Korsakov (1844-1908)

Jesu, Joy of Man's Desiring
from Cantata No. 147

19

Radetzky March

21

Cancan

from the opera "Orpheus in the Underworld"

Allegro

Jacques Offenbach (1819-1880)

23

Habanera
from the opera "Carmen"

Georges Bizet (1838-1875)

25

Toreador Song
from the opera "Carmen"

Georges Bizet (1838-1875)

O Sole Mio

Slowly, with feeling

Eduardo di Capua (1864-1917)

William Tell Overture
from the opera "William Tell"

Gioacchino Rossini (1792-1868)

Jesu, Joy of Man's Desiring
from Cantata No. 147

Johann Sebastian Bach (1685-1750)

optional: double LH 8vb

Radetzky March

Tempo di marcia

Johann Strauss (1804-1849)

23

Cancan
from the opera "Orpheus in the Underworld"

Jacques Offenbach (1819-1880)

Habanera
from the opera "Carmen"

Georges Bizet (1838-1875)

29

Toreador Song
from the opera "Carmen"

Georges Bizet (1838-1875)

O Sole Mio

William Tell Overture
from the opera "William Tell"

Gioacchino Rossini (1792-1868)

Great Music at Your Fingertips